Who Was
Jackie Robinson?

son?

By Gail Herman
Illustrated by John O'Brien

Grosset & Dunlap
An Imprint of Penguin Group (USA) Inc.

For Bennett, Lizzie, Sam, and Jeff—GH
For Linda—JO

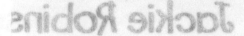

GROSSET & DUNLAP
Published by the Penguin Group
Penguin Group (USA) Inc., 375 Hudson Street, New York, New York 10014, USA
Penguin Group (Canada), 90 Eglinton Avenue East, Suite 700,
Toronto, Ontario M4P 2Y3, Canada (a division of Pearson Penguin Canada Inc.)
Penguin Books Ltd., 80 Strand, London WC2R 0RL, England
Penguin Group Ireland, 25 St. Stephen's Green, Dublin 2, Ireland
(a division of Penguin Books Ltd.)
Penguin Group (Australia), 250 Camberwell Road, Camberwell, Victoria 3124, Australia
(a division of Pearson Australia Group Pty. Ltd.)
Penguin Books India Pvt. Ltd., 11 Community Centre,
Panchsheel Park, New Delhi—110 017, India
Penguin Group (NZ), 67 Apollo Drive, Rosedale, North Shore 0632, New Zealand
(a division of Pearson New Zealand Ltd.)
Penguin Books (South Africa) (Pty.) Ltd., 24 Sturdee Avenue,
Rosebank, Johannesburg 2196, South Africa

Penguin Books Ltd., Registered Offices:
80 Strand, London WC2R 0RL, England

Library of Congress Control Number: 2010022831

ISBN 978-0-448-45557-0   10

Contents

Who Was
Jackie Robinson?

JULY 23, 1962: NATIONAL BASEBALL HALL OF FAME AND
MUSEUM, COOPERSTOWN, NEW YORK

Jackie Robinson stepped
up to a mic, not home
plate. He wore a suit
and tie, not a
baseball uniform.
At forty-three
years old, Jackie
had been retired
from the Brooklyn
Dodgers for five
years. Yet the
crowd cheered
as loudly as if he'd

just hit a World Series home run.

Jackie faced the smiling crowd. About two thousand people had gathered on Main Street in Cooperstown, New York. They were sitting and standing on the lawn in front of the National Baseball Hall of Fame and Museum. Jackie's mother, wife, and children were there. So was Branch Rickey. He had hired Jackie. Many people who didn't know Jackie had also traveled long distances to see him enter the Baseball Hall of Fame.

Jackie felt proud and grateful. Growing up, he never thought something like this could happen to him. He thanked everyone: "all of the people," he said, "throughout this country who were just so wonderful."

Baseball is a game of highs and lows, streaks and slumps. It's a tough sport, and it was tougher for Jackie than for any other ballplayer of his time. Why?

Jackie Robinson was black. In 1947, when he joined the Brooklyn Dodgers, he was the first and only African American on the team. No other major league team had black players. It was an all-white sport. And it had been that way for more than fifty years.

When Jackie was growing up, blacks and whites did not have the same chances in life. And in baseball? No blacks played on National or American League teams. Many people thought black athletes didn't have the talent, drive, or smarts.

Jackie proved these people wrong and made history. Now, in Cooperstown, Jackie was making history again. He was the first black baseball player to enter the Hall of Fame. The plaque for Jackie listed all of his amazing stats. However, there was nothing about being the first black player. Jackie hadn't wanted any mention of that. He wanted the plaque to honor his ability, the same way it did for every other Hall of Famer.

But there was no denying it—Jackie Robinson changed sports history. He was not only a baseball hero. He was a civil rights hero, too.

JIM CROW LAWS

IN SOUTHERN STATES, BLACKS AND WHITES MOSTLY LIVED SEPARATE LIVES. THERE WERE MANY RULES ABOUT WHERE BLACK PEOPLE COULD AND COULD NOT GO. THEY COULDN'T GO TO SCHOOL WITH WHITES. THEY COULDN'T EAT IN "WHITES ONLY" RESTAURANTS OR DRINK FROM "WHITE" WATER FOUNTAINS. EVEN IF BLACKS PAID FOR FIRST-CLASS TICKETS ON A TRAIN, THEY HAD TO SIT IN A SPECIAL CAR. THESE RULES WERE CALLED JIM CROW LAWS. MOST LIKELY, THE NAME "JIM CROW" CAME FROM A CHARACTER IN AN OLD SONG-AND-DANCE SHOW. JIM CROW WAS A FOOLISH, GRINNING CLOWN, MADE UP WITH A BLACK FACE.

Chapter 1
Born in the South

On January 31, 1919, Jack Roosevelt Robinson was born in the town of Cairo, Georgia. For a black family, living in the Deep South was tough. Jackie's grandparents had been slaves. His parents farmed land as sharecroppers. That meant they didn't own their small piece of land. A white farmer did. Jackie's mother and father would plant and hoe and harvest the crops. Then they had to give part of their earnings to the farmer. There was never much money left over.

MACK, JACKIE, MALLIE, EDGAR, WILLA MAE, FRANK

Jackie was the youngest of five children. Brothers Edgar, Frank, and Mack came first. Then sister Willa Mae was born, and, finally, Jackie.

There were many mouths to feed. Life got tougher when Jackie's father walked out the door and never came back. Now his mother, Mallie, had to care for her children and run the farm all by herself.

The 1920s were a scary time to live in Georgia if you were black. There were race riots. White people burned down black churches and schools. Mallie wanted her children to be safe. She wanted them to feel equal to everyone and anyone—no matter their skin color.

What could she do? Where could Mallie find a better life for her kids?

Mallie had relatives in southern California. She'd heard things were different there for black people. So she packed up all the family belongings.

Jackie was only sixteen months old when the Robinson family boarded a train that would take them all the way across the country. At midnight, the number fifty-eight train headed west.

The trip took more than a week! Finally the Robinsons passed through Los Angeles. It was nighttime. Lights were glowing up and down the mountainsides. Mallie thought it was so beautiful. She had only three dollars in her pocket. But she had hope.

Chapter 2
A New Home

Mallie found work as a maid. She also took on cooking and cleaning jobs. Soon she was able to buy a house in Pasadena, ten miles from Los Angeles.

All the Robinsons' neighbors were white. And most weren't happy when the family moved in. Some even tried to make the Robinsons leave. They called the police when the children played in the street. "Too noisy," they said.

Other kids sometimes called Jackie names. Once, when he was eight years old, a white girl shouted the most hateful word Jackie knew right at him. He wasn't afraid to answer back.

Mallie always stood up for her family. But she was calm and polite. Over time, the neighbors

grew to respect Jackie's mom. The family settled
in. They grew fruits and vegetables in the yard.
Mallie sat in a rocking chair on the front porch
and told stories.

Even in California, Jackie knew there were
rules blacks had to follow. He was only allowed

to use the city's swimming pool one day each
week. He had to sit high up in the balcony at the
local movie theater.

Because Mallie worked such long hours, often
Jackie's sister, Willa Mae, took care of him. She
was only two years older. Still, she bathed young
Jackie, fed him, and dressed him.

When Willa Mae started kindergarten, she

took Jackie along. He'd sit in the sandbox outside the school. Willa Mae would watch him through a window. She made sure her little brother didn't get into trouble.

Finally the day came when Jackie could go to school, too. Right from the start, his classmates saw how fast he ran. Kids—black and white—always wanted Jackie on their teams.

"He always had a ball in his hand," Willa Mae once said.

In dodgeball, for example, Jackie would twist and turn, avoiding the ball. He always ended up the winner.

When Jackie was about eleven, times grew more difficult for millions of families in the United States. It was the Great Depression.

Businesses were failing. People were out of work. It was harder than ever for Mallie Robinson to make a living.

Trying to help, Jackie took odd jobs. He had a paper route. He mowed lawns. But always, always, he wanted to play ball. And he wanted to win.

"He liked to be the best, and he would be unhappy at school the day we lost," a childhood friend said once. "Others would shrug it off. Not Jack."

Chapter 3
All-Around Athlete

As a teenager, Jackie was quiet and uneasy around people he didn't know well. Jackie felt closest to his older brothers Frank and Mack. "Frank was always there to protect me when I was in a scrap," Jackie once wrote. "Even though I don't think he could knock down a fly."

Mack inspired Jackie. While Jackie was still young, Mack was already a star athlete in track and field. Even when a doctor told Mack he had heart trouble, Mack kept training. And he kept getting better.

Jackie had a tight circle of friends, too. They called themselves the Pepper Street Gang. All the boys were from poor families. They were all looking for something to fill their time.

They'd swipe fruit from local stands. They'd throw dirt at passing cars. Sometimes they'd take golf balls from a golf course, then sell them back to the players. It wasn't right, but the boys never did anything violent or got into big trouble.

Even with a strong mother like Mallie, it was hard for Jackie to grow up without a dad. Men from the neighborhood stepped in to help guide Jackie. One told Jackie being in a gang was just following the crowd. Jackie listened. Then the minister of his church gave Jackie a place to go

after school. Now he didn't have to hang out on street corners. And, of course, he had sports.

By high school, Jackie was playing sports year round. He was a star athlete in track, basketball, football, and baseball. Jackie could do it all. Reporters wrote about him in local papers. The *Pasadena Post* put a big picture of Jackie on the front page of its sports section.

He wasn't the only Robinson in the news.

In August 1936, Jackie and his family sat close by their radio, listening to the Summer Olympics broadcast from Berlin, Germany. Mack had made

the US track team! He was running in the 200-meter dash.

Jackie heard the starting gun. He listened to the race, second by second. Jesse Owens, another African American from the United States, came in first place and broke the world record. Less than half a second behind him was Mack Robinson. Mack won the silver medal!

It was an amazing moment. The US almost
hadn't gone to the Olympics at all that year. Some
Americans wanted to protest against Germany.
At the time, the country's leader was Adolf Hitler.
He thought people with "pure, German blood"
were better than all others. Hitler hated Jews and
people who weren't white. Now, right in Berlin,
in the 200-meter dash, two black men had beaten
everyone else!

Jackie felt inspired to run faster and try harder.
But he saw, too, that a medal couldn't get a black
man far in the real world. After the Olympics,
Mack returned home. The excitement was over.

The only job Mack could get was as a street sweeper.

Could sports offer a brighter future for Jackie? He wasn't sure. But he did know that playing sports was what he loved most.

Chapter 4
College Star

All through high school and college, Jackie kept on making headlines in every sport he played.

In 1939, not long after he started classes at the University of California, Los Angeles (UCLA), tragedy struck. His beloved brother Frank died in a motorcycle accident.

"It was hard to believe he was gone, hard to believe I would no longer have his support," Jackie later wrote. He threw himself into sports even more. It helped to take his mind off missing Frank.

While playing basketball at UCLA, Jackie led the Pacific Coast Conference in scoring for two years in a row.

One coach called him "the best basketball player in the United States."

Jackie excelled in college football, too. "He is probably the greatest ball carrier on the gridiron today," wrote one sportswriter.

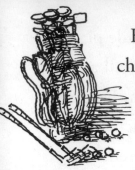

He also won golf and tennis championships. One of Jackie's dreams was to compete, like Mack had, in the Summer Olympics. But in 1940 German forces were invading other countries in Europe. World War II was raging. The Olympics were called off. There'd be no medal for Jackie Robinson.

Chapter 5
Ready for Change

During his second year at UCLA, Jackie met Rachel Isum. Rachel was a nursing student. She knew all about Jackie Robinson. Every student did.

He must be conceited, Rachel thought, *the way he stands on the field with his hands on his hips.* But as they got to know each other, Rachel discovered Jackie was almost shy.

The two had a lot in common. They both went to church. They didn't like parties or staying out late.

Jackie had never felt comfortable talking about himself. With Rachel it was different. He could tell her anything.

Not long before graduation, he told her that he didn't think a diploma was going to help him find a good job. As for sports, no blacks played on professional football, baseball, or basketball teams.

Jackie was eager to earn some money to help his mother. So he left UCLA and began coaching at a job training center. But the program soon ended.

After that, Jackie played semipro football in Honolulu, Hawaii. But when the season ended, Jackie was out of work again.

He missed his home. He missed Rachel. One week later, Jackie was on a ship heading from Honolulu back to California.

On December 7, while playing cards, he
noticed crew members painting the ship's
portholes black. The captain called everyone on
deck to explain: Dark glass made the ship harder
to spot at night.

Japanese planes had just bombed a naval base near where Jackie had been playing football for months! It had been a surprise strike, and traveling was dangerous.

At Pearl Harbor, twenty-one ships in the US fleet were sunk or damaged. A total of 2,403 people died. Now the United States joined forces with Great Britain and France. America was at war.

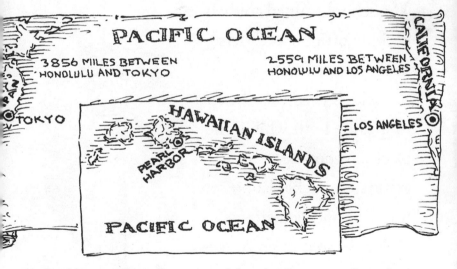

Jackie made it home safely. And soon after that, he had a new job. Jackie Robinson was drafted into the US Army.

Chapter 6
Army Days

In April 1942, Jackie was sent to Fort Riley, Kansas, far from Rachel and his family. There, he was accepted into Officer Candidate School. The school trained soldiers to become officers—leaders in the army.

Jackie's class was the first to include both whites and blacks. When he graduated, Jackie Robinson was a second lieutenant.

He wanted to go overseas. But an ankle injury prevented that from happening. He was next

sent to Fort Hood in Texas. The base had
separate quarters for blacks and whites, separate
dining halls, and separate bathrooms. The old
Jim Crow laws were alive and well.

One day Jackie was sitting on an army bus
with a friend's wife. The woman looked white,
though she wasn't. Suddenly the white driver
stopped the bus. He didn't like the idea of a black

man sitting with a white woman. He ordered
Jackie to move to the back of the bus.

"Leave me alone!" Jackie shouted back. The
driver warned there'd be trouble and called for
the military police.

Indeed there was trouble. Jackie was put on trial. At the trial, Jackie talked about his grandmother, what she'd taught him about being a slave, and what it felt like to be called nasty names.

He was found innocent.

Not long after, Jackie was sent to an army base in Kentucky. There, he met a soldier who had played baseball in the Negro Leagues. In the

1940s, there were more than two hundred all-black teams with players every bit as good as players in the major leagues.

The soldier said there was good money in playing on an all-black baseball team. In fact, the Kansas City Monarchs were looking for players.

KANSAS CITY MONARCHS

Football, not baseball, was probably Jackie's first love, and his strongest sport. Still, playing sports and making a decent living sounded good to him. On November 24, 1944, when Jackie left the army with an honorable discharge, he had a spot on the Kansas City team.

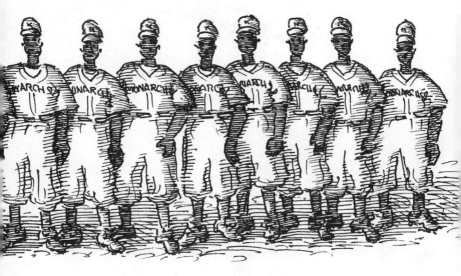

Chapter 7
The Monarchs and the Negro Leagues

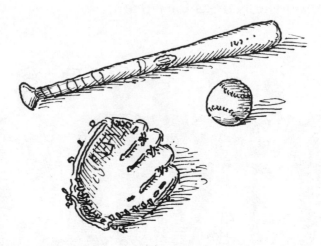

Jackie Robinson hadn't played baseball in years. Without a single day of practice, he was thrown into a game, playing shortstop for the Monarchs!

The Negro League games were very popular all through the Depression. Tickets were cheap.

The players were amazing. The games were exciting.

But the Negro Leagues didn't have as much money as the National League or the American League. For example, teams couldn't pay for spring training. Spring training gives players a chance to get in shape and improve their game. Black players had to gain skills during real games.

The Monarchs were one of the best Negro League teams. To Jackie, though, it didn't seem professional. Also, he felt he didn't fit in. He knew he had a lot to learn from the other players. He tried his best. Still, he kept to himself. And he missed Rachel a lot.

In the Negro Leagues, life on the road was rough. Teams never stayed in the same city for more than a day. In some places, there were no black hotels. Players had to sleep on the bus or outside in the ballpark.

Once, the team bus stopped for gas in
Mississippi. That was okay. But the white owner
wouldn't let the men use the restroom. Jackie
stepped forward. He told the Monarchs' driver
not to fill the tank. They could buy gas

somewhere else. The owner didn't want to lose
money. He backed down and opened the restroom.

By late August, Jackie was wondering what to
do next. He didn't know it, but one of his dreams
was about to come true!

STARS OF THE NEGRO LEAGUES

SATCHEL PAIGE (1906-1982)

SATCHEL PAIGE IS REGARDED AS THE BEST PITCHER IN NEGRO LEAGUE HISTORY. SOME WOULD SAY HE'S THE BEST PITCHER EVER. HE PLAYED FOR A NUMBER OF NEGRO LEAGUE TEAMS—INCLUDING THE MONARCHS WITH JACKIE ROBINSON. ONE SEASON, PAIGE PITCHED SIXTY-FOUR CONSECUTIVE SCORELESS INNINGS. FINALLY, IN 1948, HE BECAME THE OLDEST ROOKIE IN THE MAJORS, PLAYING FOR THE CLEVELAND INDIANS. HE WAS ELECTED INTO THE HALL OF FAME IN 1971.

JOSH GIBSON (1911-1947)

JOSH GIBSON STANDS AS ONE OF THE BEST CATCHERS AND POWER HITTERS IN ALL OF BASEBALL. HE WAS KNOWN AS THE "BLACK BABE

RUTH." FANS WHO SAW BOTH PLAYERS SOMETIMES CALLED RUTH THE "WHITE JOSH GIBSON." GIBSON NEVER MADE IT TO THE MAJORS. HE DIED AT THIRTY-FIVE, JUST THREE MONTHS BEFORE JACKIE ROBINSON BROKE THE COLOR BARRIER. GIBSON WAS VOTED INTO THE HALL OF FAME IN 1972.

JAMES THOMAS "COOL PAPA" BELL (1903-1991)

COOL PAPA BELL PLAYED CENTER FIELD IN THE NEGRO LEAGUES. HE IS CONSIDERED THE FASTEST MAN IN BASEBALL—EVER. FANS CLAIMED TO SEE HIM SCORE FROM FIRST BASE ON A BUNT. ONE TIME, ANOTHER STORY GOES, HE WAS CALLED OUT AS HE SLID INTO SECOND BASE AFTER GETTING HIT BY THE VERY BALL HE'D JUST BATTED. HE WAS VOTED INTO THE HALL OF FAME IN 1974.

AS MORE BLACK PLAYERS JOINED MAJOR LEAGUE TEAMS, THE NEGRO LEAGUE GAMES COULD NO LONGER DRAW BIG CROWDS. BY 1950, THE ERA HAD ENDED.

Chapter 8
Game Change

The Monarchs were playing at Comisky Park, the famous Chicago ball field. Jackie was out warming up when a white man waved him over.

He was a scout looking for new players to join the Brooklyn Dodgers.

That season the Dodgers had finished third in the National League. Somehow, it seemed like the team was always struggling. In fifty-five years, they'd only been in three World Series and had never won. The team's president, Branch Rickey, wanted to turn the Brooklyn Dodgers into a powerhouse team.

The scout told Jackie that Branch Rickey wanted to meet him. He was thinking of starting a new Negro League team. "Why only me?" Jackie asked the scout. After all, a new team would need lots of players. Still, he said yes to the scout. Maybe there was something bigger on Branch Rickey's mind.

Jackie took the train to Brooklyn, New York. On August 28, 1945, he stepped into Branch Rickey's office. The men stared at each other. Branch Rickey asked, "Do you have a girl?"

"Yes," Jackie said. "I do."

Why did Branch Rickey ask that question? He

wanted to know if Jackie was likely to settle down and have a family. To Branch Rickey, that said a lot about a man.

"Do you know why you were brought here?" the Dodger president continued.

Jackie said he heard there might be a new Negro League team.

Then Branch Rickey said no. Jackie was brought to talk about playing for the Brooklyn ball club.

"Me?" Jackie said. He couldn't believe it!

Rickey had made up the story about a new black team because he didn't want newspaper reporters finding out the Dodgers were interested in a black player. It would make headlines. And Rickey wanted to make changes quietly. His plan was for Jackie to start playing for the Dodgers' minor league team in Montreal. They were called the Royals. Good players in the Royals moved up to the Brooklyn Dodgers. That was Rickey's hope for Jackie.

THE BROOKLYN DODGERS

WHERE DID THE NAME FOR BROOKLYN'S MAJOR LEAGUE TEAM COME FROM? IN THE EARLY 1900S, TROLLEY TRACKS RAN IN CRAZY PATTERNS THROUGH THE STREETS OF BROOKLYN. PEOPLE HAD TO "DODGE" THE TROLLEYS AT EVERY TURN. BROOKLYN FANS HAD THEIR OWN NAME FOR THE TEAM, "DEM BUMS." EACH YEAR THE EXCITEMENT WOULD BUILD . . . WOULD THE DODGERS WIN THE PENNANT? WOULD THEY WIN THE WORLD SERIES? AND THEN . . . DISAPPOINTMENT. ALTOGETHER, THE TEAM WOULD PLAY IN NINE WORLD SERIES.

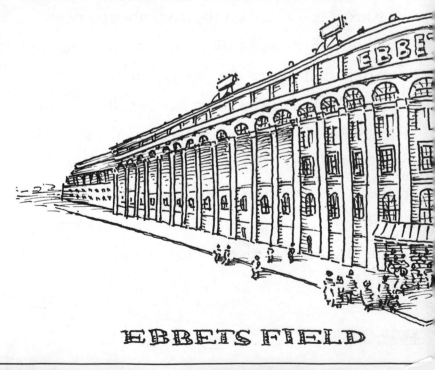

EBBETS FIELD

BUT THEY'D WIN ONLY ONCE, IN 1955, WITH THE
DREAM TEAM OF PEE WEE REESE AND JACKIE
ROBINSON IN THE INFIELD, DUKE SNIDER IN
CENTER FIELD, CARL FURILLO IN RIGHT FIELD, ROY
CAMPANELLA BEHIND HOME PLATE, AND DON
NEWCOMBE PITCHING. "WAIT TILL NEXT YEAR," THE
LOYAL FANS SAID EACH YEAR. THEY WERE USED
TO HEARTBREAK. BUT THEY FINALLY GAVE UP
HOPE—ONCE AND FOR ALL—IN 1958. THAT'S WHEN
THE TEAM LEFT BROOKLYN AND MOVED TO
LOS ANGELES.

BROOKLYN, NEW YORK

After hearing what Branch
Rickey said, Jackie couldn't say a
word. This was really happening!
He was thrilled, scared, and excited all at the
same time.

He knew he wanted to do it—for black people
everywhere—but also for his mother, for Rachel,
and for himself.

Finally he managed to say one word: "Yes."

Branch Rickey believed in equality. But he
knew there'd be problems with white players who
didn't want to play with Jackie and with white
players who didn't want to play against him. Some
white fans and white umpires wouldn't welcome
Jackie, either. Jackie's temper would be tested
again and again.

Branch Rickey was very direct. What would
Jackie say when someone called him names? What
would Jackie do if a player dug his cleats into
Jackie's leg on base? Or threw a pitch at his head?

"Mr. Rickey," Jackie finally said. "Do you want a ballplayer who's afraid to fight back?"

"I'm looking for a ballplayer with guts enough *not* to fight back," Rickey said.

Jackie understood. All black people would be judged by how he behaved. If he lost control, it would hurt the chances of other black players hoping to join the majors.

Jackie *did* have the guts not to fight back.

Before he left the building, he had signed up with the ball club.

Chapter 9
Spring Training

In early 1946, Jackie was almost twenty-seven years old. It was a time of big changes. On February 10, Jackie married Rachel. A few weeks later, the newlyweds left for spring training in Daytona Beach, Florida.

Jackie felt scared and excited. Now he was playing for the Montreal Royals. The next step could be the major leagues! Jackie understood that being the first black player would be difficult. In fact, just getting to Florida for spring training was a struggle.

The Robinsons flew from L.A. to New Orleans. They had to catch a connecting flight to Pensacola, Florida, then on to Jacksonville. But

they were bumped from flight after flight because they were black. They couldn't find an airport restaurant to eat in. They were for "whites only."

When they finally reached Pensacola, Jackie and Rachel once again were bumped from flights. White people got the seats instead. So they decided to take a bus the rest of the way. They had to sit in the "for coloreds" back row, the worst seats on the bus. The trip took one-and-a-half days.

No matter how tired he felt, Jackie knew he had to be at his best for the first day of training. He walked onto a field with two hundred players. Everyone on the Montreal team was white, except for one black pitcher named Johnny Wright. He was also trying out, but all eyes were on Jackie.

Reporters were there, too. "What would you do if one of these pitchers threw at your head?" one asked.

"I'd duck!" Jackie answered.

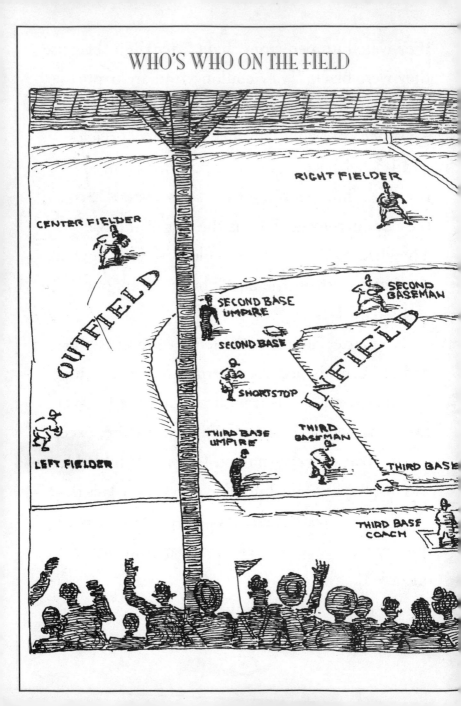

Jackie tried to joke when asked questions like this. But often it was hard to keep a sense of humor. Jackie couldn't stay at the same hotel as the other players. He and Rachel had to stay at the home of a local couple.

Sometimes other teams canceled games. They refused to play against a black player. Some ballparks locked their gates from Jackie and the rest of the Montreal players. Once, a game in DeLand, Florida, was called off. The excuse was that the stadium lights weren't working. But it was a daytime game. No lights were needed.

Some players on his own team looked through Jackie like he wasn't even there.

At times Jackie was so fed up, he wanted to go home. But he didn't. He kept on practicing and playing.

It wasn't all bad.

Crowds poured into the stands to watch Jackie bat and try out his new position. Sure, some people came to jeer. But many more people came to cheer. The black sections overflowed. Fans had to be turned away.

When spring training was over and the Royals returned to Montreal, Jackie was their second baseman.

Johnny Wright was signed up, too. He wasn't expected to play. He was on the team so Jackie had someone to room with on the road.

April 18, 1946, was opening day. Jackie and the Royals were in New Jersey playing their first regular season game against the Jersey City Giants.

People flooded to the stadium. Bands played. Music filled the streets. It was the first baseball season since World War II had ended, and it was a huge event.

Jackie was second in the lineup. There was already one out when he stood at the plate. His hands were sweaty. His legs felt weak. Nervous, Jackie grounded out to the shortstop. But he'd done it. He'd hit the ball at his first at bat.

Two Montreal Royals were on base for his second at bat. Everyone thought Jackie would

bunt to move the players forward. The pitch came high and fast. Jackie swung. *Crack!* The ball sailed over the left field fence out of the park. It was a three-run homer!

In the fifth inning, Jackie stole second . . . then advanced to third . . . then ran on to home. The crowd roared. Thanks to Jackie, the Royals won 14–1.

By the end of the game, even Jersey City fans were cheering for Jackie. The clubhouse was mobbed with fans and reporters. Everyone wanted to congratulate the daring new player.

How did Jackie feel? One reporter wrote that
Jackie "was so excited he had to tie his necktie
three or four times, but he was as happy as a kid
on Christmas morning."

Chapter 10
The Minors

Jackie and Rachel liked living in Montreal. Their neighbors were friendly and helpful to Rachel, who was expecting a baby.

Life on the road often wasn't so nice. One time in Syracuse, New York, a player on the other team threw a black cat onto the field. "There's your cousin!" he called to Jackie.

Jackie remembered what Branch Rickey told him. So he said nothing. Instead, he waited to come up to bat. Jackie doubled, then ran home on the next single. Playing great baseball was the best way to prove he belonged on the team.

It was thrilling for fans to watch him play. He hit the ball hard. He was a master at stealing bases. Jackie led his team to the Little World Series. Just like the World Series, whoever won in a best of seven series would win the Minor League Championship.

The Royals were playing the Louisville Colonels. For the first time, southern Kentucky was hosting an integrated baseball game. The fans there were loud and mean. Jackie did not play his best. After three games, the Royals were down two games to one.

But everything changed back in Montreal for Game 4. Jackie scored the tying run. Then in extra innings, he drove in the winning run. In the next game, Jackie doubled and tripled. In the eighth inning he bunted, bringing home a man on third. The Royals won 5–3.

The Royals won Game 6, too, *and* the series—thanks to two double plays by Jackie and two big hits. Fans screamed their hearts out for Jackie. People streamed onto the field and carried him on their shoulders.

The next month, Jackie celebrated another event: His son Jackie, Jr., was born on November 18th in a Los Angeles hospital.

For a little while, Jackie relaxed and enjoyed his family. He loved spending time in California with his mother, brothers, and sister. But in just a few months, Jackie would be back at spring training. Now was the time to prove he was ready for the majors.

Chapter 11
The Majors

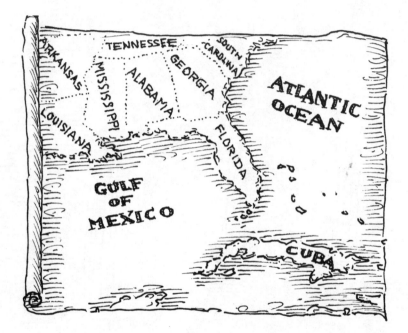

In 1947, spring training for the Dodgers and the Royals was in Cuba, an island ninety miles off the coast of Florida. Jackie had grown to feel comfortable with the Montreal players. But even in Cuba Jackie had to stay in separate housing and eat in different restaurants from his teammates.

Because the Dodgers already had many shortstops and second basemen, Jackie was now told to try a new position—first base.

Jackie understood. Switching to first baseman gave him a better shot at making the Dodgers team, but it wasn't easy learning a new position. It also didn't help Jackie's focus that rumors were flying: First Jackie was on the Dodgers. Then he was off. Then he was on again.

LEO DUROCHER

Leo Durocher, the Dodgers' manager, saw how talented Jackie was. One night he called a meeting at the hotel. Although it was late, he pulled all the players from their rooms. Jackie wasn't there. Durocher had heard some Dodgers were banding together to try to keep Jackie off the team. In a now famous speech, Leo Durocher announced, "I don't care if a guy is yellow or black, or if he has stripes like a zebra. I'm the manager of this team, and I say he plays."

Jackie was going to get the Dodgers into the World Series, Durocher told his players. After that, none of the players talked about keeping Jackie off the team.

Finally, on April 10, 1947, Jackie met with

Branch Rickey again and got the news he wanted to hear: He was a Dodger! Still, Rickey asked him to play one last time as a minor leaguer.

That afternoon, Jackie played his last game as a Royal against the Dodgers at an exhibition game in Brooklyn. In the sixth inning, Jackie bunted into a double play.

At the same time, a news announcement was handed out to reporters. It was a short announcement, but it made sports history. A black player was in the majors!

Jackie Robinson was a Brooklyn Dodger.

Chapter 12
Number 42

Five days later, on April 15, 1947, Jackie played in his first major league game. The Dodgers were at home at Ebbets Field in Brooklyn.

One newspaper headline read: "Triumph of Whole Race Seen in Jackie's Debut in Major League Ball." Talk about pressure!

It was a cool, clear afternoon. When Jackie reached the clubhouse, he put on his #42 uniform for the first time.

"It fit me," Jackie said later, "but I still felt like a stranger, or an uninvited guest."

Jackie knew Rachel, with Jackie, Jr., was cheering from the stands. And he knew his mother was rooting for him, too, back in California. That helped him stay calm as he took first base.

The Dodgers were playing the Boston Braves. The Braves were up first. The first Braves batter hit a ground ball to third. The third baseman picked it up and tossed it to Jackie. Out!

Two outs later, the Dodgers trotted off the field. At Jackie's first at bat, the crowd cheered. He held the bat high. He leaned into his stance, toes pointing in. Holding his Louisville Slugger tightly, he faced the pitcher.

Curveballs and fastballs came at Jackie like

speeding bullets. Hard, high-speed strikes. This wasn't the minors anymore.

Finally, Jackie swung. The ball arched, then rolled toward third. It was an easy out. Still the crowd cheered.

The Dodgers won 5–3. But Jackie was disappointed. He wanted to play better. He hoped to be a key part of the team.

In the early days, Jackie was quiet around his teammates. He kept to himself. Nobody, he felt, was trying to make him feel wanted. Jackie kept telling himself it didn't matter if no one liked him. All that mattered was respect.

Jackie received threatening letters from people he didn't know. One said, "We have already got rid of several like you," in block letters. Some letters threatened to harm Rachel and Jackie, Jr. Branch Rickey showed them to the police.

Players on other teams pointed bats at Jackie like machine guns. They dug their cleats into him as they stepped on first base.

The first game against the Philadelphia
Phillies was very tough on Jackie. The Phillies
shouted such hateful insults that Jackie later said,
"[they] brought me nearer to cracking up than I
ever had been." But there was an upside. His
Dodger teammates stood up for him. Second
baseman Eddie Stanky shouted back at the

Phillies, "You yellow-bellied cowards. Why don't you yell at somebody who can answer back?"

Sometimes, Jackie wanted to throw down his bat and raise his fists. He didn't. He just tried to play the best baseball he could. And his game got better.

Bit by bit, Jackie relaxed both on the field and off. He and Rachel found a place to live in Brooklyn. He began to joke with his teammates. He joined their card games.

The captain of the Dodgers was shortstop Pee Wee Reese. At first he kept his distance from Jackie. That changed during a game in Cincinnati.

Fans yelled at Pee Wee to stop playing with Jackie. He was a southerner after all. He should know better, they said.

Pee Wee didn't even glance at the stands. He walked over to Jackie and put his hand on his shoulder. The yelling stopped, and a friendship began.

More and more, Jackie became an important member of the Dodgers. Patient at bat, he waited for the right pitch. And when he reached first, he'd dance around the base.

Pitchers eyed him nervously. They knew he had lightning speed. Would Jackie try and steal? Would he stay put? Pitchers paid more attention to Jackie than to the batter. And before anyone knew it, there'd be a hit and the runners would advance.

Jackie stole bases like no one had before. And the fans loved it.

Piles of fan letters for Jackie Robinson poured

into the clubhouse. Fans crowded the stands. They roared at every home game. Rachel was always there, too. And Jackie's game just got better and better.

What a season! Jackie's success was even greater than Branch Rickey thought possible. *Time Magazine* put Jackie on its cover. He was named Rookie of the Year—the first one ever. The Dodgers won an outstanding ninety-four games. The team took the pennant, with Jackie leading the league in stolen bases.

Now it was onto the World Series, playing against the American League champs, the Yankees. Mallie Robinson took her first airplane flight to be there, along with Mack, Willa Mae, and Rachel's mom.

The series went the full seven games. In the end, the Dodgers lost. But for Jackie, the year felt like a victory. After the last game, every teammate came to his locker to say good-bye.

Every one shook his hand. He was part of the team.

BROOKLYN DODGERS

1947

Chapter 13
Glory Years

Jackie played for the Dodgers for ten years. During those years, he and Rachel had two more children, Sharon and David. They moved from Brooklyn to a house in Queens, and then to a bigger house in Connecticut.

Jackie wrote two books about his life.

He starred in a movie, *The Jackie Robinson Story*.

With Jackie, the Dodgers won six National League pennants. Time and again they went up against the Yankees in famous "Subway Series." Time and again, they lost.

The year 1949 was Jackie's greatest season. He was named Most Valuable Player and led the National League in hitting and stolen bases.

A year later, Branch Rickey left the Dodgers. It was a blow to Jackie, who thought of Rickey almost as a father.

Times were changing. Slowly, more black players were being signed to major league teams. Don Newcombe and

DON NEWCOMBE
PITCHER BROOKLYN DODGERS

Roy Campanella both joined the Dodgers. They became All-Stars, too. The Cleveland Indians and the St. Louis Browns both signed black players soon after Jackie Robinson broke the color barrier.

During those years, the civil rights movement grew stronger. People fought for blacks to be treated fairly. Even though Jackie was the highest-paid Dodgers player of all time, in the South he still couldn't stay in the same hotels as his white teammates.

As time went on, Jackie decided that he had kept his promise to Branch Rickey. Now he could speak up off and on the field.

Jackie began to shout at umpires. He talked back to rival teams. Some people thought he was

ROY CAMPANELLA
CATCHER BROOKLYN DODGERS

too loud. But others defended him. They said
Jackie was doing what any player would do. It
was just making news because of his color.

In 1955, Jackie was thirty-six years old. He
was turning gray and losing speed. He was
playing outfield now. People thought his best
days were over.

Once again, the Dodgers were facing the
Yankees in the World Series. And in the very
first game, something amazing happened—

Jackie Robinson stole home, right under the glove of catcher Yogi Berra!

It was a hard-fought series that went to a
seventh game. Jackie sat that one out.

Game 7 turned out be a Dodgers victory. The Brooklyn Bums had won their first World Series! And how sweet that it was against the Bronx Bombers!

THE YANKEES

IN 1913, A TEAM CALLED THE HIGHLANDERS MOVED TO THE BRONX AND WAS RENAMED THE NEW YORK YANKEES. WHEN BABE RUTH JOINED THE TEAM SEVEN YEARS LATER, THE YANKEES BECAME THE STRONGEST TEAM IN BASEBALL—AND "THE BRONX BOMBERS" HAVE BUILT ON THAT LEGACY EVER SINCE. THEY'RE THE TEAM OTHER FANS LOVE TO HATE.

BABE RUTH

WHY? THEY'VE WON MORE CHAMPIONSHIPS THAN ANY TEAM IN ANY SPORT EVER. SOME OF THE MOST FAMOUS NAMES IN BASEBALL HAVE WORN THE YANKEES PINSTRIPES: BABE RUTH, LOU GEHRIG, JOE DIMAGGIO, AND MICKEY MANTLE, JUST TO NAME A FEW. TO THIS DAY, THE YANKEES ARE THE TEAM TO BEAT.

JOE DI MAGGIO

Chapter 14
Beyond Baseball

The following year, 1956, Jackie was traded to the New York Giants. But Jackie had already decided to retire. He was tired of the travel. He wanted to be closer to his family. Jackie, Jr., was ten, Sharon was six, and David was four. He wanted to be home for dinner.

Plus he wanted to devote a lot more time to civil rights. He also became involved in politics. In 1963, he marched in Washington, D.C. with Martin Luther King, Jr.

THE CIVIL RIGHTS MOVEMENT

ALTHOUGH THE CIVIL WAR (1861-1865) ENDED SLAVERY IN THE UNITED STATES, MANY AFRICAN AMERICANS STILL DID NOT HAVE THE SAME RIGHTS AS WHITE PEOPLE 100 YEARS LATER. THEY WERE OFTEN TURNED AWAY FROM GOOD JOBS, FROM BUYING HOUSES IN WHITE NEIGHBORHOODS, AND EVEN FROM VOTING. THE CIVIL RIGHTS MOVEMENT PUSHED TO STOP THESE INEQUALITIES.

THE 1963 MARCH ON WASHINGTON WAS AN IMPORTANT MOMENT IN THE CIVIL RIGHTS MOVEMENT. MORE THAN 250,000 PEOPLE GATHERED AROUND THE REFLECTING POOL NEAR THE WASHINGTON MONUMENT WHERE MARTIN LUTHER KING, JR., GAVE HIS NOW FAMOUS "I HAVE A DREAM" SPEECH.

ON JULY 2, 1964, PRESIDENT LYNDON JOHNSON SIGNED THE CIVIL RIGHTS ACT OF 1964 INTO LAW. IT MADE SEGREGATION IN PUBLIC PLACES ILLEGAL, SPELLING AN END TO THE OLD JIM CROW LAWS OF THE SOUTH.

Jackie, along with his family and thousands of others, held a peaceful protest for equal rights.

Dr. King and Jackie admired one another greatly. "He is a legend in his own time," Martin Luther King, Jr., said of Jackie.

Jackie was busier than ever. He worked for the National Association for the Advancement of Colored People (NAACP). He helped found an African American–owned bank. He started a company to build houses for poor families.

Jackie kept breaking color barriers: He was the first black vice president of a major American company. He was the first black TV analyst for major league baseball. Meanwhile, Rachel kept busy, too. She received another degree from New York University and became an assistant professor at Yale University School of Nursing.

Mallie Robinson lived to see all these successes. But she collapsed outside her Pepper Street home in Pasadena in 1968. By the time Jackie arrived in California, she had passed away. Jackie gazed at her still face and realized she had died in peace.

Year after year, Rachel and Jackie made a difference in people's lives. But Jackie's health was failing. The same year he retired, doctors told Jackie he had diabetes, a kidney disease. He had heart problems, too.

Even harder for him to bear were his son's problems. Jackie, Jr., fought in the Vietnam War. When he returned home, he was addicted to drugs. It took time, but Jackie, Jr., managed to kick his addiction. In fact, he was working as a drug counselor when he died in a car accident. He was just twenty-four years old.

That same year, 1972, the nation celebrated Jackie and the Brooklyn Dodgers again. It was the twenty-fifth anniversary of Jackie Robinson

breaking the color barrier. On October 15, Jackie threw out the first pitch at the World Series. Just as they had before, fans cheered and rose to their feet for Jackie Robinson. It was a glorious moment.

Nine days later, Jackie died at home. He was fifty-three years old.

Chapter 15
The Legend Lives On

Forty-six years after Jackie was voted into the Hall of Fame, a new plaque went up in his honor. The plaque noted his great skills in the sport of baseball. But this time, it also paid tribute to Jackie's bravery.

At the ceremony, Rachel Robinson spoke. She said she knew that Jackie would approve of the change.

The plaque now reads:

Jack Roosevelt Robinson
"Jackie"
Brooklyn, N.L., 1947–1956

A player of extraordinary ability renowned for his electrifying style of play. Over 10 seasons hit .311, scored more than 100 runs six times, named to six All-Star teams and led Brooklyn to six pennants and its only World Series title, in 1955. The 1947 Rookie of Year and the 1949 N.L. MVP when he hit a league-best .342 with 37 steals. Led second basemen in double plays four times and stole home 19 times. Displayed tremendous courage and poise in 1947 when he integrated the modern major leagues in the face of intense adversity.

After his death, Jackie Robinson received the Presidential Medal of Freedom. The award honors people who have made our country better. Helen Keller, Neil Armstrong and

the Apollo 11 astronauts, and President John F. Kennedy have all received the medal, too.

To continue Jackie's work, Rachel started the Jackie Robinson Foundation in 1973. The foundation helps young people stay in school and go to college. To this day, the foundation is going strong.

Fifty years after Jackie broke the color barrier, his number, forty-two, was retired from both the National and American Leagues. In 2004, April 15, the date of his first game for the Dodgers, was named Jackie Robinson Day. To honor Jackie, every player on every team wore the number forty-two. Jackie Robinson Day is still celebrated today.

And today more than one-third of major league ballplayers are men of color. But it all started with one brave man: Jackie Robinson.

JACKIE'S STATS

THIS CHART LISTS STATISTICS FROM JACKIE'S YEARS PLAYING BASEBALL WITH THE BROOKLYN DODGERS IN THE MAJOR LEAGUES. IT DOES NOT INCLUDE STATISTICS FROM HIS YEARS PLAYING WITH THE NEGRO AND INTERNATIONAL LEAGUES.

YEAR	BATTING AVERAGE	GAMES PLAYED	HITS
1947	.297	151	175
1948	.296	147	170
1949	.342	156	203
1950	.328	144	170
1951	.338	153	185
1952	.308	149	157
1953	.329	136	159
1954	.311	124	120
1955	.256	105	81
1956	.275	117	98
TOTAL	.311	1382	1518

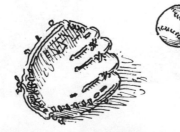

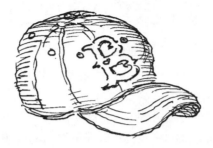

HOME RUNS	RUNS BATTED IN	STOLEN BASES
12	48	29
12	85	22
16	124	37
14	81	12
19	88	25
19	75	24
12	95	17
15	59	7
8	36	12
10	43	12
137	**734**	**197**

TIMELINE OF
JACKIE ROBINSON'S LIFE

1919 — Jack Roosevelt Robinson is born in Cairo, GA

1920 — Robinson family moves to Pasadena, CA

1939 — Jackie enrolls in UCLA
Brother Frank dies in motorcycle accident

1941 — Jackie plays football for the Honolulu Bears

1942 — Jackie is drafted into the US Army

1945 — Jackie joins the Kansas City Monarchs
Jackie signs a contract to play for the Montreal Royals

1946 — Jackie marries Rachel Isum
Son Jackie, Jr., is born

1947 — Jackie becomes the first black player on a modern
major league baseball team

1949 — Jackie is named MVP of the National League

1950 — Daughter Sharon is born

1952 — Son David is born

1955 — Brooklyn Dodgers win their first World Series

1957 — Jackie retires from baseball

1962 — Jackie is voted into the National Baseball Hall of Fame

1971 — Jackie, Jr., dies in a car accident

1972 — Jackie dies on October 24

1973 — Rachel Robinson starts the Jackie Robinson Foundation

TIMELINE OF THE WORLD

First nonstop flight across the Atlantic Ocean takes sixteen hours and twelve minutes — **1919**

Nineteenth Amendment to the Constitution gives women the right to vote — **1920**

New York Stock Market crashes — **1929**

Empire State Building opens in New York City — **1931**

Germany invades Poland and World War II begins — **1939**

Japanese planes bomb Pearl Harbor and US enters World War II — **1941**

Anne Frank and family go into hiding in Amsterdam — **1942**

World War II ends — **1945**

Chuck Yeager pilots first plane to travel faster than the speed of sound — **1947**

Korean War begins — **1950**

Polio vaccine is announced — **1955**
Disneyland opens in California
Montgomery Bus Boycott is held to end segregation

John F. Kennedy becomes first Catholic president — **1961**

Beatlemania hits the US — **1964**

Thurgood Marshall is appointed to the US Supreme Court, becoming the first black Supreme Court Justice — **1967**

Martin Luther King, Jr., is assassinated in Memphis, Tennessee — **1968**

Title IX is signed into law, giving girls and boys equal opportunities in all school programs, including sports — **1972**

BIBLIOGRAPHY

*Driscoll, Laura. **Negro Leagues: All-Black Baseball**. New York: Grosset & Dunlap, 2002.

Eig, Jonathan. **Opening Day: The Story of Jackie Robinson's First Season**. New York: Simon & Schuster, 2007.

*O'Connor, Jim. **Shadow Ball**. New York: Alfred A. Knopf, 1994.

*Prince, April Jones. **Jackie Robinson: He Led the Way**. New York: Grosset & Dunlap, 1997.

Rampersad, Arnold. **Jackie Robinson: A Biography**. New York: Alfred A. Knopf, 1997.

Robinson, Jackie, as told to Alfred Duckett. **I Never Had it Made: An Autobiography of Jackie Robinson**. New York: HarperCollins, 1995. Originally published, New York: Putnam, 1972.

*Robinson, Sharon. **Promises to Keep: How Jackie Robinson Changed America**. New York: Scholastic, 2004.

Tygiel, Jules. **Baseball's Great Experiment: Jackie Robinson and his Legacy**. New York: Oxford University Press, 1983.

*Starred books are for young readers.